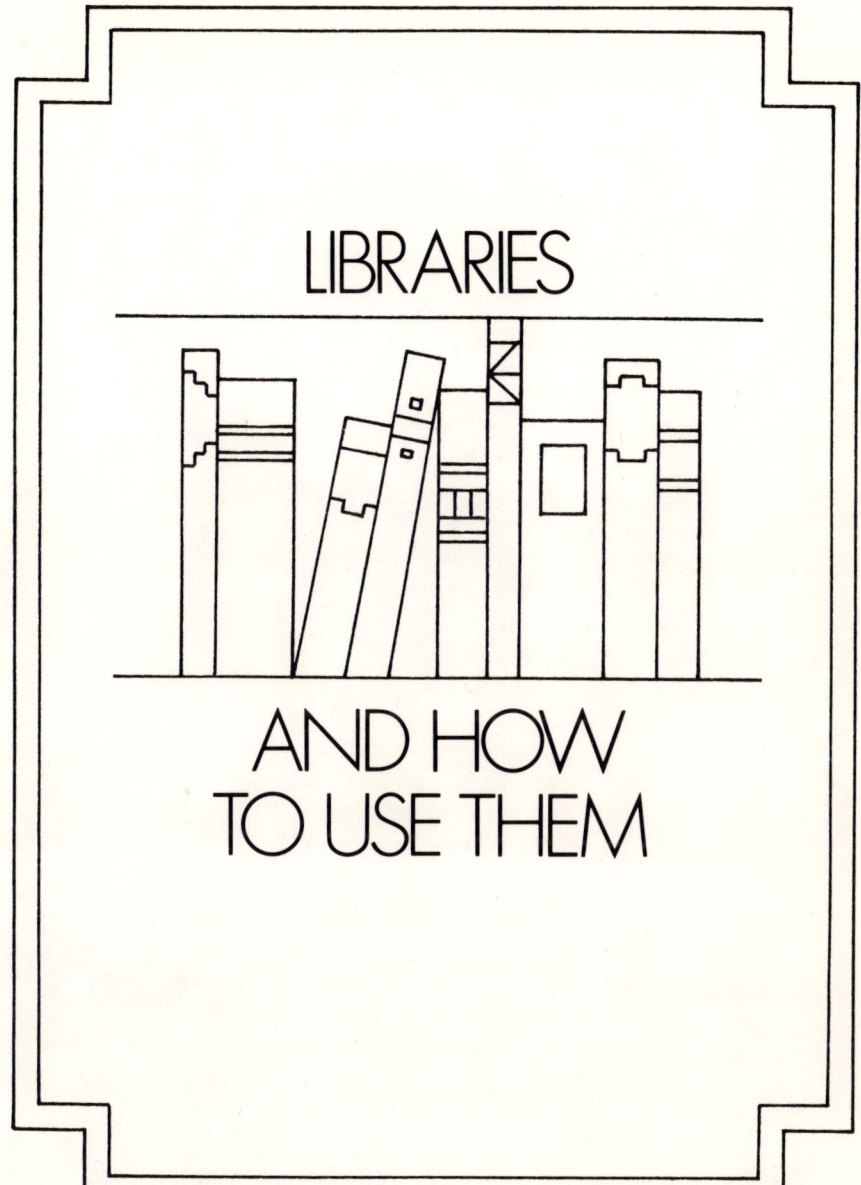

LIBRARIES

AND HOW TO USE THEM

BY JEANNE B. HARDENDORFF

FRANKLIN WATTS
NEW YORK | LONDON | 1979
A FIRST BOOK

021
H

Photographs courtesy of: The New York Public Library Picture Collection: pp. 3 (above and below), 4; The Library of Congress: pp. 6 (inset), 29, and 30; The Harvard University News Office: p. 6; Historical Society of Pennsylvania: p. 7; John Youngblood/Boulder Public Library and the American Library Association: p. 12; United Press International: pp. 13 and 49; Culver Pictures: p. 21; The American Library Association: p. 40.

Library of Congress Cataloging in Publication Data

Hardendorff, Jeanne B
   Libraries and how to use them.

   (A First book)
   Includes index.
   SUMMARY: An introduction to libraries and the use of their resources, including reference books, catalogs and the Dewey Decimal and the Library of Congress classification systems.
   1. Libraries—Juvenile literature. [1. Libraries] I. Title.
Z665.5.H37   021   78-12992
ISBN 0-531-02259-5

Copyright © 1979 by Jeanne B. Hardendorff
All rights reserved
Printed in the United States of America
5 4 3 2

CONTENTS

CHAPTER ONE
What are Libraries?
1

CHAPTER TWO
The Dewey Decimal
Classification System
17

CHAPTER THREE
The Library of Congress
Classification System
27

CHAPTER FOUR
The Library's Catalog
35

CHAPTER FIVE
So You Want to
Borrow a Book
47

CHAPTER SIX
Reference Books and
How to Use Them
51

INDEX
59

Libraries are storage bins for all the collected knowledge and wisdom of the world. In the United States today there are over 87,000 libraries, many for public use.

Modern libraries have deep roots in the past. But they have developed and changed a great deal over the centuries, in order to better fill the needs of those who use them.

ORIGINS

Archaeologists have uncovered libraries of clay tablets five thousand years old, in what was the ancient land of Mesopotamia. These clay "books" were inscribed with a symbolic language called **cuneiform.** Almost as long ago, the ancient Egyptians began to draw symbolic messages on a thin paper-like fiber called **papyrus.** Later, papyrus sheets were pasted together and rolled up into scrolls that look a lot like window shades. Sometimes 100 feet (29 m) long, these scroll "books" began to be collected into libraries. One very large such library was founded in Alexandria, Egypt, by Ptolemy I, the ruler of Egypt, in 332 B.C.

In the second century B.C., specially treated animal skins began to be used in the making of books. This material, called **parchment,** was strong enough to be sewed together into sheets. Also, both sides could be written on. Thus the book, as we think of it today, actually began then.

The ancient Romans, during the first four centuries A.D., established many libraries throughout their realm. They used both

Above: a Babylonian spelling book, dating back to 442 B.C. Below: a fragment of Egyptian papyrus.

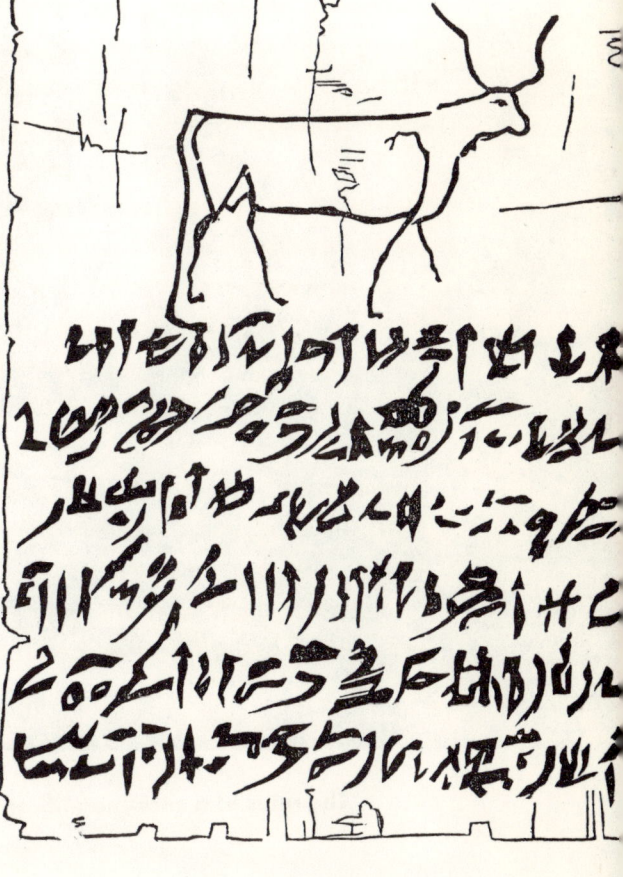

The ruins of a once-magnificent library in the ancient world.

papyrus scrolls and parchment. The parchment sheets were bound together in book form and called **codexes.**

Gradually, the use of papyrus died out. Because the papyrus decayed so quickly, not many papyrus scrolls survived to today. One scroll library that did survive was found in the ruins of the city of Pompeii. The library had belonged to a nobleman. Pompeii had been destroyed, and the library buried, when the volcano on Mount Vesuvius erupted in 79 A.D.

During the Dark and Middle Ages, almost all of the books produced were done on parchment and were completely handwritten. They were usually kept in monastery or university libraries or in the homes of wealthy nobles or special societies. The books produced were for the very few who could read in those times — philosophers and scholars mostly — never for the general public. With the printing of a book by movable metal type in 1456, everything began to change. Books could be produced much faster. In the three centuries that followed, libraries grew in number and size all over Europe.

In America, many private or semi-private libraries were established during the 1700s, though some, such as the one at Harvard College, had been established a little earlier. But most of the early libraries had been formed for the use of a particular group, such as an historical society.

During the 1700s many American libraries opened to the public. But the user had to pay a fee to join the library. The Library Company of Philadelphia, founded by Benjamin Franklin in 1731, was one of the first of this type.

The Public Library of Peterborough, New Hampshire, appears to have been the first public library to have been supported through taxation. It was established by vote in April, 1833, and

Inset: Gutenberg's printing press (1456) revolutionized the printing industry. Left: Harvard University's first library was the earliest ever built in America. Today, it is America's largest university library, housing over 8½ million volumes of written material. The Harry Elkins Widener Memorial Library, shown here, is Harvard Library's principal building.

Above: an artist's view of the old Library Company of Philadelphia, founded in 1731 by Benjamin Franklin.

provided free library services to the community. This date then marks the beginning of the steady growth of large and small free public libraries in the United States.

LIBRARIES TODAY

Many things about libraries have changed. They once were dark and gloomy places, where no one spoke above a whisper. Now most of them are full of light and are arranged to make those who use them feel welcome.

Also, today, there are many different kinds of libraries. Each kind offers a particular service. Let's look at some of the different types.

PUBLIC LIBRARIES

The word public comes from a Latin word, *publicus*, meaning people. A public library is for all the people in a community to use. It charges no fee for its services. The public library will have available, within the limits of its budget, a wide variety of books and other materials. These books or other materials may be **borrowed,** or taken out for a specified time, by anyone in the community — the business person or the artist, the pre-schooler or the grandparent. The library **loans** its materials.

Public libraries are usually tax-supported. There are a few that are instead supported from money that has been donated. And there are some that receive part of their money from taxes and part from gifts.

Few public libraries are exactly alike. Not only are the shapes and sizes of the buildings different, but so are the number of books and other materials in each. Your nearest library may be like the Los Angeles (California) Public Library, which has over 4,538,458 books and bound periodicals (magazines and journals) in its collection. Or it may be like the Cherokee County (Alabama) Public Library, which has only about 3,800 books in its collection.

Libraries vary in other ways, too, for instance in the number of hours (or days) they are open or in the number of people who work there. Most public libraries, however, arrange their books and other materials in similar ways. They divide their collections into two basic age groupings, children and adult (adult includes young adult). Adult books are in one place; children's books are in another. Then the books are further separated by the *kind* of book. Storybooks — works of **fiction** — are separated from information, or fact books — **nonfiction.**

People often want to refer to, that is, look something up, in a certain basic information book. Thus **reference books,** which are rarely read cover to cover, are put in a special place in the library, a reference section or perhaps a reference room (in larger libraries). Reference books are never to be taken out of the library building.

Each library decides for itself how it should further arrange its books and other materials. In a large city library, certain nonfiction material may be put into a special area or separate room. For instance, there may be a separate room just for all the material a library has on music. In another large city, the music material might not be kept so separate. It would depend on what the people in that city had indicated they found useful.

A library's **holdings** are everything the library has in its collection. These holdings almost always reflect the community's special interests. Suppose, for example, there were a town where Morgan horses were widely raised and trained. That town's library would most likely have a great deal of material about Morgan horses: books and perhaps films on how to raise and train these horses, and material on the history of the breed. Since the people who were interested in Morgan horses would probably be less interested in other breeds of horses, the library might have only a small amount of material on mustangs or appaloosas.

How does a library develop a good collection for the community it serves? One important way is by librarians listening to what local residents ask for and then adding the proper material to the collection.

Any library requires a certain amount of money in order to operate. Part of the money goes to buying books and other materials. Some goes to paying the salaries of the library staff. As mentioned earlier, libraries get their money from taxes. Most towns support their own public libraries. However, in some rural areas the towns are too small to raise enough tax money to support a public library. In these cases there is usually a "county" library instead. The county library will serve a number of towns and villages. When two or more counties join together to offer library service, they form one type of "regional" library. The First Regional Library of Mississippi, for example, serves four separate Mississippi counties. Large cities often have "branch" libraries. That is, there are a number of libraries scattered around the city, but all operate as part of one library system. Each is called a "branch" of that city's library.

Many public libraries — town, county, or regional — operate a **bookmobile,** often called a "library on wheels." A bookmobile is a truck with bookshelves inside. With such a vehicle, library services can be taken to different parts of a city, or to rural areas where there is no library building.

Public libraries often send a staff member with books and magazines to hospitals and nursing homes that don't have their own libraries.

In communities where there are no school libraries, or where the school libraries are quite small, the public library may loan collections for use in the classroom.

When a public library does not have a book or something else you need in its own collection, it will try to borrow that material from another library. *Inter* is a Latin word that means between. A loan from one library to another is called an **interlibrary loan.** Libraries frequently lend each other materials.

What public libraries have available to loan has changed through the years. Books and magazines, of course, are the mainstay of almost all libraries. But now most libraries also have records, tapes, films, and film equipment available. Many have framed paintings and prints or photographs you can borrow. And you may even live near a library that will lend you a real live animal!

Many public libraries also run programs that can teach or just entertain you. These include story hours and film showings. They might also include demonstrations, such as how to make puppets, build model airplanes, or weave your own basketball net. Usually a bulletin board in the library will list special events. It is a good idea to always check there to find out what's happening in your library.

SCHOOL LIBRARIES

School libraries differ from public libraries in one basic way. Each school library provides library services only to its own students and teachers, not to the community as a whole. School libraries

Left: today, libraries lend all sorts of things to their patrons. This little boy is "borrowing" a rabbit for a week.
Above: this children's librarian is conducting a story hour for a group of pre-schoolers in Albany, New York.

are there to help students with what they are learning in school and doing in their free time. Thus the school librarian must always be aware of what goes on in class and what the children enjoy doing when not in class. It is the library's job to help the student go beyond what he or she learns in class or from textbooks.

Because they contain so many different kinds of materials for learning, such as films, records, even board games and photographs, many school libraries are now called **media centers, resource centers,** or **learning centers.**

Your school library may be one that is open before classes start and after classes have finished. There are some school libraries that are only open during regular school hours. Check the bulletin board or ask the librarian for a schedule.

COLLEGE AND
UNIVERSITY LIBRARIES
There are nearly 3,000 colleges and universities in the United States. Each has at least one library. Some have more than one, such as one for each major division of the school — law, medicine, engineering, and so on. A few university libraries have collections of **rare books.** These books are used by students and scholars in research projects. They are considered rare because they are very old, or perhaps because there are only a few copies of that book available anywhere.

SPECIAL LIBRARIES
A special library is one that concentrates on collecting materials that will best serve the needs of a particular group of people. Banks and zoos, museums and manufacturers, medical societies and race-track associations are but a few such groups. Each group

has its own limited area of interest and stocks its library with specialized types of information.

STATE LIBRARIES

Each of the fifty states, plus the territories of Guam, the Virgin Islands, and Puerto Rico has a State Library. These libraries may serve a number of purposes. All act as reference libraries for state lawmakers. Some also help develop library service throughout their particular state. For instance they may advise a town that has never had a library on how to start one. State libraries also often conduct courses for librarians and assistants who have not been otherwise trained.

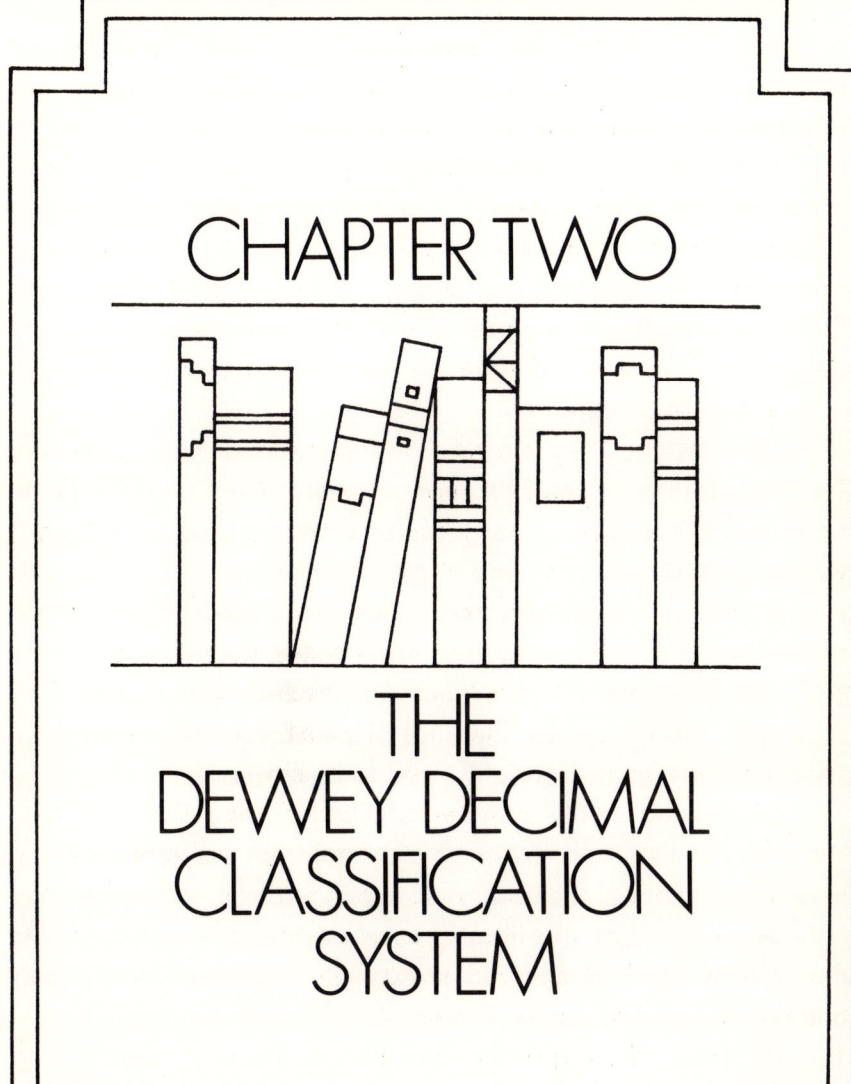

If you have used your school or public library already, you have probably noticed that the books are marked with numbers and letters, usually on the book's spine. These numbers and letters are repeated on a **book card** inside. What does it all mean?

Every library has a **classification system,** a way of organizing its books and other materials. These systems were designed to help the users of the library and the library staff itself find what is in the library's collection and where it is to be found. Each classification system has its own set of marks, or **notations,** as they are called. The numbers and letters in the notation might be thought of as a form of shorthand.

Libraries also keep a record of every item in their collection. This record, called a **shelf list,** not only tells where each item is to be found, but also how many copies there are of each, where it was bought, what it cost, and much, much more.

A library is organized very much like a grocery, where different brands of similar products are on open shelves in the same area. For example, all pet foods are close together, and then separated into groups by the kind of pet. Frozen foods are kept separate from foods that don't need to be frozen.

Organizing in this manner is called *putting like with like.* Libraries put like with like in several different ways. Books that may be taken out of the library are separated from those that may only be used inside the library, such as reference books. Books that will be used by children are usually separated from books that will be used by adults. Fiction is separated from nonfiction.

A library, like a grocery, has shelves. Rows of freestanding bookshelves are called **stacks.** Today, most public and school libraries have *open* stacks. This means that you yourself can take from the shelves what you want to look at or borrow. Some parts of some large public libraries have *closed* stacks. When the stacks are closed, the borrower must wait until someone on the staff gets the desired item.

To classify means to arrange or organize according to class or category. We saw how a grocer uses a system to group pet foods together, to make it easier for the shopper to find what he or she wants.

A classification system in a library serves a similar purpose. **Biographies,** that is, books about people's lives, are grouped together. A nonfiction book about snakes is put with other nonfiction books about snakes.

There are two major classification systems used in libraries today. One is called the **Dewey Decimal Classification System (DDC).** The other is called the **Library of Congress Classification System (LC),** and is discussed in some detail in the chapter following this one. Both systems, though different, put nonfiction books on the same subject together.

Before the DDC and LC systems were created, some libraries classified their books by size. For over a hundred years, the Library Company of Philadelphia classified books this way. There were four sizes of books. The sizes were given Latin names that referred to how many times the standard printer's sheet (19 by 25 inches or 48 by 62 cms) had been folded. As a book was added to the collection, it was also given a number. This number merely indicated in what order the book had been added. Thus, if a library had ten books of various sizes about horses, and each had been added to the collection on a different day, then to find all the books on horses, one would have to look in ten separate places!

There were other systems in use at this time too. Some libraries, for example, numbered each shelf and then numbered each book to indicate it was book 8 or 15 for shelf 3333. Other libraries arranged their books alphabetically by the last name of the author. Today, most libraries still arrange their fiction books this way. But for nonfiction, this system didn't work too well. Any book written by a person named Brown would be shelved with all the other books written by people named Brown. Thus, a book about the pharaohs of Egypt could sit between a book about gardening and a book about medicine.

It became possible to change from those awkward methods of classifying with the creation of the Dewey Decimal System.

From 1870 to 1874, Melvil Dewey was a student at Amherst College in Massachusetts. He worked part-time there in the college library. The library used one of the classification systems just described. Books on the same subject were to be found in many different places.

Dewey strongly believed that everything should be done in a way that would save time. As a boy, he had even devised a system for arranging the pantry in his home in a certain order. Later in life, Dewey legally shortened his birth name from Melville Louis Kossuth Dewey to Melvil Dewey. If it had been legal, he probably would have shortened Dewey to Dui!

Dewey believed that the way words were spelled should be made simpler. If he had had his way, spelling would be a lot easier for all of us. We wouldn't have to remember to add silent letters (*have* would have been *hav* and *knife* would have been *nife*). Double consonants would have been eliminated wherever they were unnecessary (notice how he changed the spelling of his

Melvil Dewey, 1851–1931

name *Melville* to *Melvil*). His favorite argument in support of a simpler spelling was that it would save time and money. Shorter, more simply spelled words would result in shorter books, which would use up less paper and less ink. Books, therefore, could be produced more cheaply and in less time.

It is not surprising that Dewey, once he began to work in the library, decided to find a better way to organize his college library's collection. That better way came to him one day in 1873.

Dewey knew the expression, "As simple as A, B, C." It suddenly occurred to him that 1, 2, 3 was even simpler.

Dewey also knew of the metric system, a system based on divisions of tens. He realized that he could use numbers and decimals in order to classify all knowledge found in books. There could be ten different "classes," or fields of knowledge. Each of the numbers 1 through 9 could stand for one of the ten different fields. The zero (0) could be used for those books that included information on a wide variety of subjects, such as a general encyclopedia.

By using the same set of numbers, 0 through 9, each of the ten classes could be carried a step further, into ten "divisions." The ten divisions could then be divided into ten "sections." Then, by the use of decimals, the sections could be subdivided even further.

Dewey felt his system was easy to learn. In 1926, he wrote, "In its simpl form a skoolboy can quikly master it and keep for instant reference not only his books but every note, clipping or pamflet."

If you want to prove he was right, here are the ten classes of Dewey's system:

```
000 — 099    Generalities*
100 - 199    Philosophy
200 - 299    Religion
300 - 399    Social sciences
400 - 499    Language
500 - 599    Pure sciences
600 - 699    Technology (applied sciences)
700 - 799    The Arts
800 - 899    Literature and rhetoric
900 - 999    General geography, history,
             and related disciplines
```

Let's look more closely at the way this works. The numbers 500–599 were assigned as the notation for what is called the Pure Sciences. Pure Sciences consist of subjects such as mathematics, physics, chemistry, and astronomy. Each of these subjects is assigned a division and a section number. For example, all books on mathematics will fall between the numbers 510 and 519.

As you may know, there are many different kinds of mathematics, including arithmetic, algebra, and geometry. The number specially assigned to geometry is 513. And there are even different kinds of geometry. By using a decimal point, books on different kinds of geometry can be classified separately — thus, the decimal part of the Dewey Decimal Classification System:

*There is no need to memorize the system in order to be able to use it. You will learn why later.

```
513.1    Plane geometry
513.3    Solid geometry
513.5    Modern geometry
```

Now, in geometry you solve problems. Books on usual or typical geometry problems are given the number 513.9. Books containing *famous* geometry problems are given the number 513.92.

Classifying a book this way is called "building a number." You start with the general subject number, then go on to get more and more specific. Each library decides for itself how specific it *needs* to be when classifying a book being added to its collection. Such flexibility is one of the great advantages of the system.

Let us suppose a new book, whose title and subject are *Piloting an Airplane*, was recently added to a library's collection. The number the book was given was 629.132 52. How was this number built?

```
629.132 52    Piloting
              is an aspect of
629.132 5     Flying and related topics,
              which is an aspect of
629.132       Principles of flight,
              which is an aspect of
629.13        Aeronautics,
              which is an aspect of
629.1         Flight vehicles and engineering,
              which is an aspect of
```

629	<u>Other branches</u> (of engineering), which is an aspect of
620	<u>Engineering and allied operations and manufactures</u>, which is an aspect of
600 - 699	<u>Applied sciences</u>, one of the ten basic classes.

Your school library may classify its copy of *Piloting an Airplane* as 629.132 52. However, if there is not much apparent interest in the subject, and the library does not anticipate that it will ever have a very large selection of books on the subject, it could use just 629.1 and stop there.

The Dewey Decimal Classification System is the one you are most likely to find in an elementary, junior high, or high school library, and in many public libraries. The other principal system used in the United States is the Library of Congress System, a description of which follows.

CHAPTER THREE

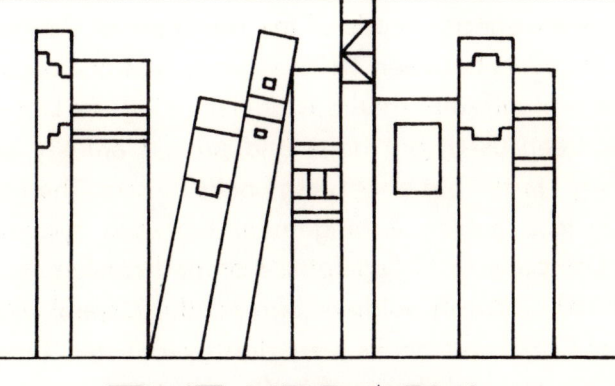

THE LIBRARY OF CONGRESS CLASSIFICATION SYSTEM

The Library of Congress Classification System developed quite differently from that of the Dewey Decimal Classification System. It was not the work of one person, but of many. It was not developed for use in other libraries, but for use in only one. The principal concern at the time it was developed was for the Library of Congress, in Washington, D.C., to have a system that would make the handling of its own collection more efficient. A system was needed that would work as well in 1997 as it did in 1897 and also serve the special needs of the members of Congress.

In the years between 1800, when it was first organized, and 1897, several different methods of classifying the Library's collection had been used, but none had proved entirely satisfactory. The Library started out classifying books by size. Then it switched, in 1812, to a subject arrangement that had appeared in the Library Company of Philadelphia's printed catalog.

In 1814, British soldiers burned the Capitol. Most of the Library of Congress's books were destroyed. Later, Thomas Jefferson sold his personal library of 6,487 books to Congress to replace the burned volumes. Jefferson had developed a classification system for use in his own library. His books were grouped in forty-four classes (he called them "chapters"). The Library of Congress continued using Jefferson's system, with some changes, for many years.

By 1897, however, the Library's collection had grown to nearly a million books. It was becoming clear that a new and more efficient system of classification would have to be found. Other classification systems that had been developed and their schemes published were considered. Among these were the Dewey system and the **Expansive Classification System** devised by a man named Charles Ammi Cutter, the librarian of the Boston Athenaeum.

The Library of Congress in Washington, D.C.

The beautiful room pictured is the main
reading room of the Library of Congress.

Cutter's system used a single letter as the notation for the subject classes. This notation could be expanded by adding one or more additional letters. The Library of Congress decided to make up its own system, using Cutter's system as a guide. The result was named the Library of Congress Classification System.

Nowadays, most university and college libraries, as well as some of the very large public libraries, use the system developed. There are still, however, a few libraries that use Cutter's original system.

Currently, there are twenty classes in the Library of Congress Classification System. The individual classes are:

```
  A:  General Works
  B:  Philosophy—Religion
  C:  History—Auxiliary Sciences
  D:  History and Topography
        (except America)
E-F:  American History
  G:  Geography, Anthropology, Folklore
        Manners and Customs, Recreation
  H:  Social sciences
  J:  Political sciences
  K:  Law of the United States
  L:  Education
  M:  Music and Books on Music
  N:  Fine Arts
  P:  Language and Literature
  Q:  Science
  R:  Medicine
```

S: Agriculture—
    Plant and Animal Industry
T: Technology
U: Military science
V: Naval science
Z: Bibliography and Library Science

In the Library of Congress Classification System, a single letter (A, H, M) is assigned to each class. Then, by using a second letter, the main class may be divided into subclasses. Finally, with the addition of numbers, classifying becomes more and more specific.

By using the alphabet, it is possible to have twenty-six subdivisions of any one class. Each of the subdivisions can be further subdivided by using the numbers 1 to 9999.

Let's see how a book about hounds gets its notation in the LC system:

The class S   = Agriculture—
                            Plant and Animal Industry

    SF   = Animal Culture
    SF 429   = Varieties of Dogs
    SF 429.H6 = Hounds

Thus, under this system, a book on hounds would have the notation: SF 429.H6.

This could also be written: SF
                                  429
                                  .H6.

The process of classifying new material, using either system discussed, is not as easy as it may seem. Suppose, for instance, that your library acquired a book about water. This seems simple enough to classify. But consider some of the many ways water can be thought of:

```
As a means of transportation—inland or oceanic
The chemical composition of water
As part of landscape architecture
Use in fire extinction
Water games and sport
Location of water by divination (dowsing)
The technique of water painting
Water pollution
Water's use in agriculture
Canal engineering
Geological tables of water
Water's importance in certain religions
```

Before the book is added to the collection, it must be read or scanned to decide how it should be classified. This is an important decision. How a book is classified will determine where it is put on the shelf and, also, how easily it can be located thereafter.

A book, once classified, with its DDC number or LC notation on its spine, is put on the shelf for library users to find. But *how* can the user locate the book?

CHAPTER FOUR

THE LIBRARY'S CATALOG

All of a library's holdings are listed in a special **catalog** kept somewhere in the library. This catalog is nothing more than a list, really. It is for your use. You read earlier that when classified, an item is given a certain notation or set of marks. That notation assigns the item its place on the shelf. The library's catalog is there to tell *you* where to look on the shelf.

A library's catalog often consists of small, separate cards kept in trays or drawers in a cabinet: hence, the name **card catalog.**

Not all libraries use cards, however. Sometimes the catalog is kept in books, the pages of which are computer-printed listings. In libraries that use even newer technologies, the catalog is put on **microfilm** or **microfiche.** When that is the case, a special magnifying viewer must be used to read the contents of the catalog.

It is possible that there is one kind of catalog in your school library and another kind in your nearest public library. But whatever kind of catalog the library you are using has, you will find it is set up much the same way as the others are.

All library catalogs are arranged alphabetically, with each item the library has listed separately. And each item is usually not listed once, but three times! Once by title, once by author, and once by subject.

Each listing in a catalog is called an **entry,** and the kind of entry it is comes from the information given on the top line. For example, an **author entry** has the author's name on the top line. A **subject entry** has the subject heading on the top line. And a **title entry** will have the book's title on the top line.

Though every library has such a catalog, the way its contents are arranged may vary. Some libraries have a *divided* catalog, other libraries have a *dictionary* catalog.

In a divided catalog, there are two separate alphabetically arranged sections. One section contains all the author and title entries. The other has all the subject entries. If you were looking up LIZARDS as a subject, you would use the section that had the subject entries. On the other hand, if you were looking up a book with the title *Lizard Music*, you would use the section with the author-title entries.

A dictionary catalog does not separate the entries. All are combined together into a single alphabetical file, similar to the way words are entered in a dictionary; hence, the name dictionary catalog. In such a catalog, LIZARDS as a subject would be in the same alphabetical file as the title entry, *Lizard Music*.

Though all catalogs are filed alphabetically, there are different ways this can be done. You may be able to see the problem if you have two different dictionaries at hand. Look up the term *witch doctor* in the first. You may find that it appears *before* the word *witchcraft*, though the letter *d* comes after the letter *c*. Then look up *witch doctor* in the other dictionary. You may find that in the second dictionary, the term *witch doctor* appears *after* the word *witchcraft*. The reason for this apparent discrepancy is that one dictionary files its words letter-by-letter, while the other chooses to file word-by-word. (Different encyclopedias, by the way, vary their filing methods in the same way.) If you are puzzled about how to use your library's catalog, ask the librarian.

Let's look now at some typical situations.

Suppose that a friend has recommended that you read a book entitled *Call It Courage*. To find if that book is in your library, you would go to the library's catalog and locate the proper section that contained listings for the letters Ca, or perhaps Cal. There will be guide words or guide letters to help you quickly locate the section of the alphabet you want. If the guide letters say A to Bar, for example, that section will contain all the listings for A, but only the B's through Bar. (You will soon see how much time you can save if you know your alphabet perfectly.) What you would be looking for in this case is the title entry. You would look through the entries until you found one that said *Call it Courage* on the top line. If there is such an entry, then you know that the library owns at least one copy of the book.

But suppose, instead, you had enjoyed reading *Little House on the Prairie*, written by Laura Ingalls Wilder, and wanted to find out if that author had written any other books. To look up an author, you always look under the author's *last name*. You would go to the catalog, but this time to the section containing the listings for Wil, and look until you found the entry or entries with the author's name — Wilder, Laura Ingalls — on the top line. Each of Wilder's books would have its own title listing.

If there are several authors with the same last name, their entries will be arranged alphabetically by their last name, then their first name. Authors with the last name of London, for example, will be filed as follows:

```
London, Arthur
London, Jack
London, Perry
```

Finally, suppose you were doing a report for your class on flying saucers, and you wanted to see what your library had on the subject. You would go again to the catalog, but this time to the section that has listings for items beginning with the letters FLY, and look until you found FLYING SAUCERS on the top line. Under the subject entry or entries, you will find all the items the library has on the topic.

If your library has a card catalog, you may notice that you can easily remove the drawers from the cabinet. They slide right out. This is useful, because it is hard to read material in drawers high up or low down. Don't hesitate to take the drawer you need out and put it on a flat surface nearby. But never remove the cards inside the drawers. Come prepared with paper and pencil to copy down the needed information. And always remember to put the drawer back in the cabinet when you've finished.

If your library has a book catalog, there may be enough duplicate copies so that you can carry one with you to the shelves as you look for the items you want. Information on the cover of this catalog will tell you what letters of the alphabet are in each book, and whether the catalog has only subject entries or entries by title or author.

If the library's catalog is on microfilm or microfiche, you will be using a magnifying viewer. A marker, off to one side, will indicate the range of listings that will appear on the viewer. Control buttons enable you to make the contents of the catalog move forward and backward. (It is an extra bonus to know the alphabet not only from A to Z, but from Z to A when using one of these catalogs.)

WHAT'S IN AN ENTRY?

Even though there may be three entries for each item the library has, there is only one **main entry.** This is usually the author entry, whether the author is a person, an organization, a government

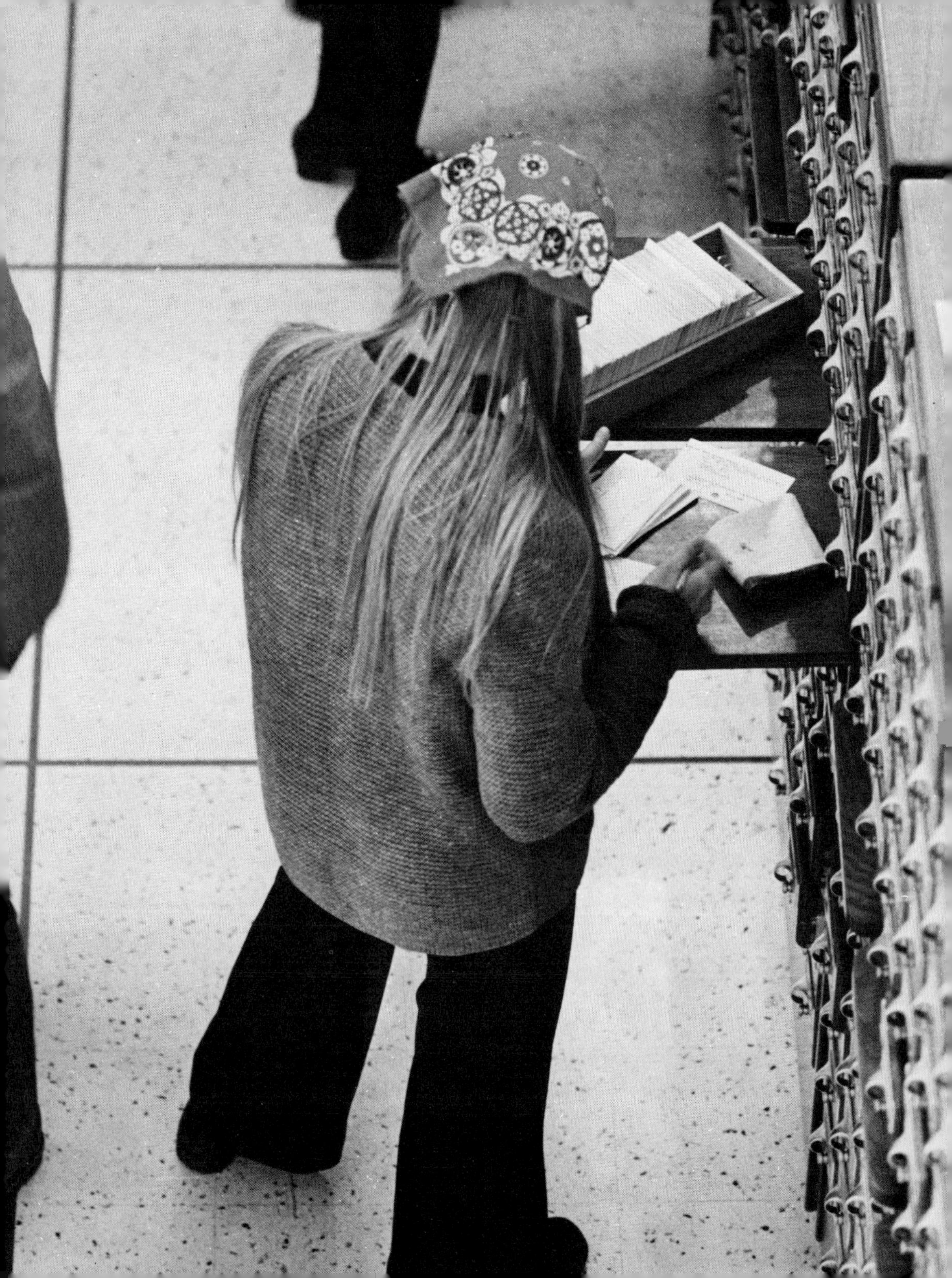

agency, or whatever. The main entry, in many libraries, will give you a great deal of information about the book. Much of this information has been taken from the title page of the work itself. On the first, or top line, of a main entry will be the author's name, last name first. Then on the next line will come the title of the work. Following this will be the place of publication, the name of the publisher, and the date of publication. Other bits of information in the entry will tell if the book is illustrated, how many pages are in the book, the size of the book, whether the book has a **bibliography** (a listing of other books and materials used by the author to create his or her book) or a **glossary** (a listing and defining of special terms used in the book).

Also for each entry, located in the upper lefthand corner, will be the LC or DDC notation. This notation, plus the author's number (a special library code for the author's last name), makes up the item's **call number.** All books and other materials are shelved by this number, and the shelves are clearly marked so that you can easily find what you want.

The term "call number" comes from the time when all libraries followed a rule similar to an 1885 rule of the Princeton (Massachusetts) Public Library and Reading Room. This rule said, in part, that "No person other than the librarian shall be allowed to take books from the shelves." To get a book under this rule, you had to "call," or request, each book by its number — never by title or author. The term has stuck to this day, though most libraries now let you get the book yourself.

Using the card catalog

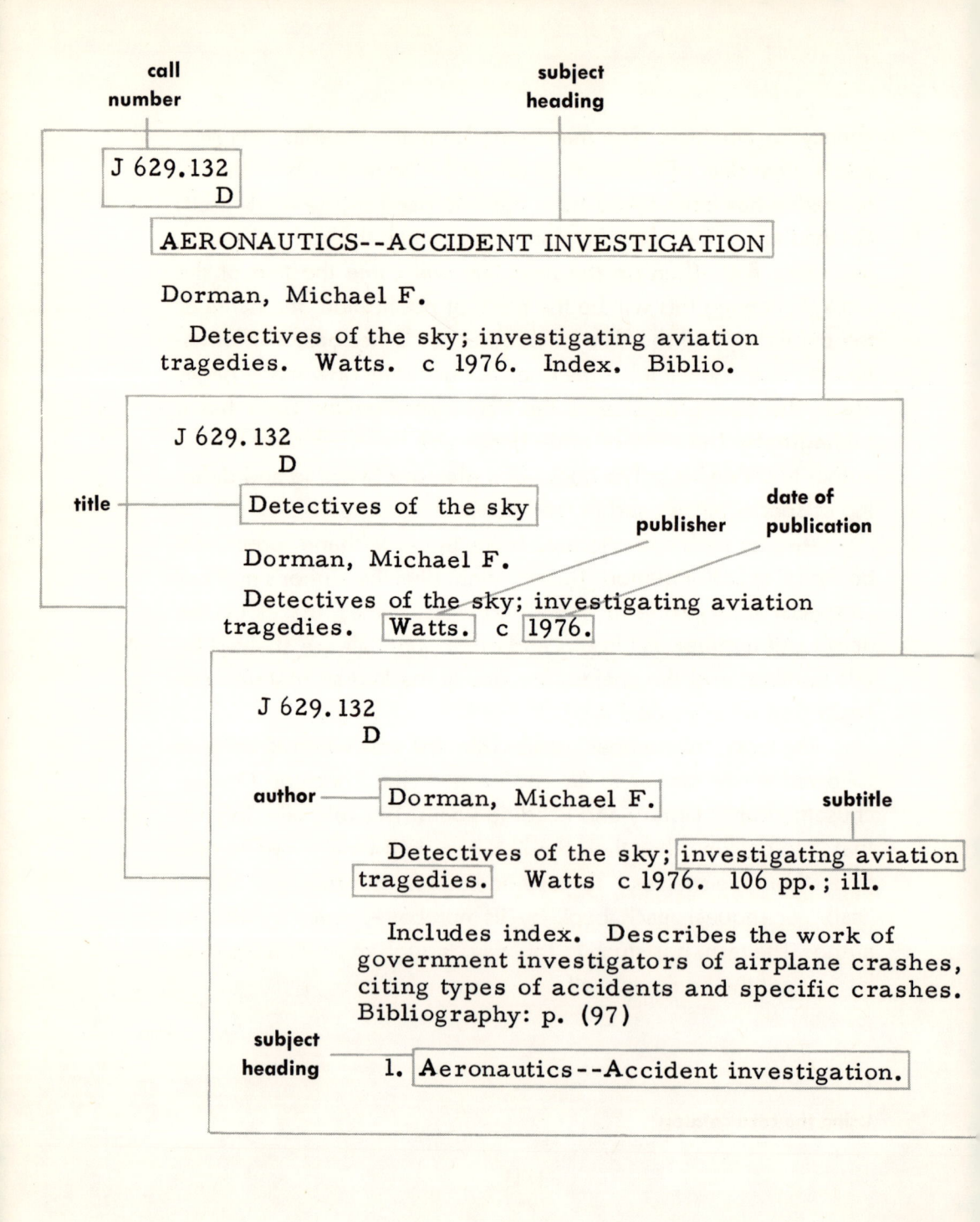

call number | **subject heading**

J 629.132
D

AERONAUTICS--ACCIDENT INVESTIGATION

Dorman, Michael F.
  Detectives of the sky; investigating aviation tragedies. Watts. c 1976. Index. Biblio.

J 629.132
  D

title — Detectives of the sky

publisher | **date of publication**

Dorman, Michael F.
  Detectives of the sky; investigating aviation tragedies. Watts. c 1976.

J 629.132
  D

author — Dorman, Michael F.   **subtitle**

  Detectives of the sky; investigating aviation tragedies. Watts c 1976. 106 pp.; ill.

  Includes index. Describes the work of government investigators of airplane crashes, citing types of accidents and specific crashes. Bibliography: p. (97)

subject heading
    1. Aeronautics--Accident investigation.

```
FIC
  J
   R
      Rockwell, Thomas

      How to eat fried worms.  Rockwell, Thomas,
   1933-  New York  c 1973.

      Two boys set out to prove that worms can make
   a delicious meal.  Illustrations by Emily
   McCully.

      (1) McCully, Emily Arnold, illus.
```

Left, top to bottom: subject entry, title entry, and author entry of a non-fiction book. Above: the main entry card for a work of fiction.

The call number is the number you should write down if you want to get the book itself. With it in hand, you go off to find the area in which the book has been shelved. Learning the general layout of the library will save you time, especially for nonfiction books. You rarely need the call number of a work of fiction if you know the author's last name. This is because fiction is most often arranged alphabetically by the author's last name, and kept separate from nonfiction.

Other entries will contain some, but not necessarily all, of the information to be found in the main entry. A title entry will have the title listed on the top line, and it will include at least the name of the author and the call number.

Each subject entry will have the subject listed on the top line with the author's name directly below, followed by the title, and again the call number in the corner. You may find many subject entries in the catalog for one subject, each of which lists a different book.

Subject entries tell you the contents of a book. The library selects terms for these entries that it feels the user will recognize. Using the subject entries will help you in another way, too. It may be the fastest way to track down a particular item (book, film, filmstrip) when you half-remember its title and aren't sure of the author's name. Whenever you have trouble finding a subject you are looking for, ask a librarian for help. You may only need to use a slightly different term or one that includes the topic you are after. If, for example, you looked up DUNGEONS but did not find such a listing, it would not necessarily mean that your library had no material on dungeons. Rather, the library may use the term PRISONS as the subject heading for its material on dungeons.

SEE AND SEE ALSO ENTRIES

Suppose you were interested in being a magician. You want to see what your library has about magic tricks. Because you are already somewhat familiar with the subject, you know that the word *prestidigitation* means "sleight of hand," and is related to magic. But would everyone know that word?

If you looked up *prestidigitation* in the catalog, you would probably find an entry like this:

```
        PRESTIDIGITATION.
             see

    CONJURING;
    MAGIC.
```

This type of entry is called a **see reference.** It refers you to the term that the library has used in classifying books on that subject.

You learned earlier that to classify a book that dealt with water required pinpointing just how the subject was treated in the book. A library's catalog shows through its **see also** entries the various aspects of a subject that can be found in the collection. A see also entry is in addition to other entries. It may be filed before or after all the other entries with the same heading. An example of a see also entry is:

POTTERY.
see also

CHINA PAINTING
also names of varieties of pottery, e.g.
DERBY POTTERY, DRESDEN POTTERY, WEDGWOOD WARE,
and subdivision POTTERY under INDIANS, INDIANS
OF MEXICO, INDIANS OF NORTH AMERICA, ETC.
TILES
URNS
CRACKLE
DECANTERS
GLAZES
GLAZING (CERAMICS)
CERAMICS

CHAPTER FIVE

SO YOU WANT TO BORROW A BOOK

Most public libraries require you to register before you are allowed to borrow any of their materials. This means you will probably be asked to fill out and sign a special registration card. When you do this, you are not only giving the library your name and address for their files, you are also signing an agreement. The agreement says, basically, that you will accept responsibility for the items the library lends you, and that you will obey the rules of the library. A parent or guardian is sometimes also required to sign the card.

To be entitled to use your school library, you probably must only be enrolled in that school.

Once you are registered, you will be issued a **library,** or **borrower's card.** On this card will be your name and a number. Each time you **check out,** that is, officially borrow something from the library, you will have to present this card to the librarian.

If your dog eats the card or you lose it, don't despair. It can be replaced. Just tell the librarian.

If your library is large enough, it may have film equipment that you may borrow. To do so, however, usually requires a separate registration. You may also have to take and pass a course the library gives on how to operate the different pieces of equipment.

You usually check out and return borrowed material at the same desk. The sign on this desk may read **Circulation Desk, Check Out Here,** or perhaps **Charge Desk.**

Microfilm viewers are found in almost all libraries today. They permit the library to house a great deal of material in just a small amount of space.

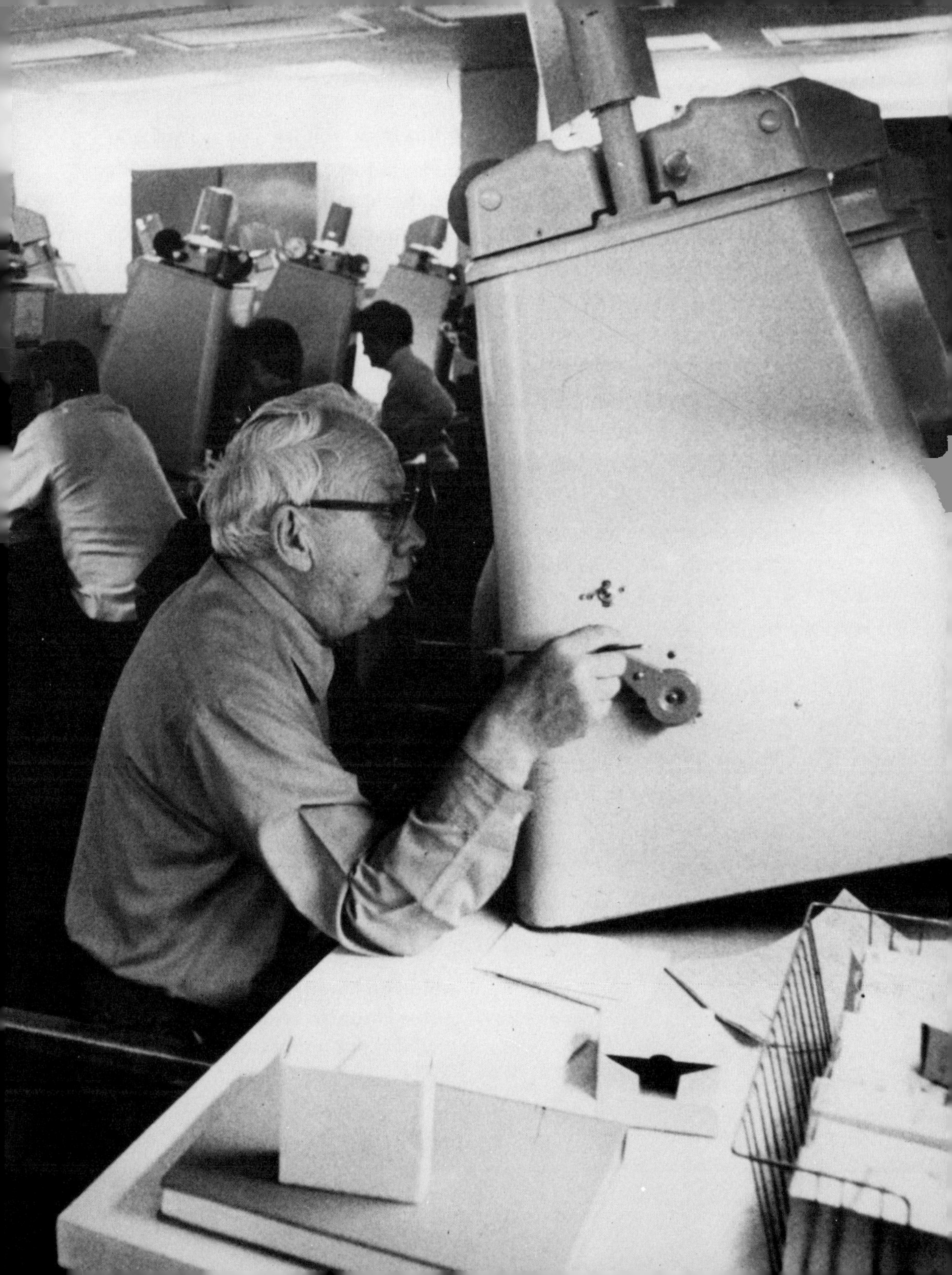

The library staff member at this desk will take your card and stamp the book card with a date. This is the date by which you are expected to return the material to the library, so others can have the chance of borrowing it. Many libraries allow you to **renew** the book — check it out again — if it has not been requested by others.

Some libraries charge a fine for each day a library book is **overdue,** kept out beyond the date stamped on the book card. There are also often fines for books returned damaged or written in. Should you lose a library book, you may be required to pay the library the amount it was worth.

Not paying fines could result in your losing all library privileges.

CHAPTER SIX

REFERENCE BOOKS AND HOW TO USE THEM

Reference materials, materials to refer to or to consult briefly for information, are thought of as tools. A tool is something you use to help you do the job at hand. A tractor and a hoe are tools for the farmer. A dictionary, an encyclopedia, and an atlas can be tools for the student doing a class assignment or just satisfying his or her curiosity.

Of course any printed matter could be considered a reference tool. But reference books are a breed all their own. They are designed for quick and easy information giving.

Each reference tool has its own organization. Before you begin to use one, familiarize yourself with it by reading its **table of contents.** This will show you what you will find in the volume or set and give you an idea of how the material is organized.

In the **preface** or **introduction,** or in a section by itself, you will find an explanation of how to use the work. If symbols are used, there will be a key that will decode them for you. Many reference works use abbreviations that are explained at the front of the book. Any limits the work has will also be described here. It may be that the subject is covered only until the year 1850, or the information given is only on those persons famous in history who were left-handed or knock-kneed.

Keep in mind, too, that the most important resource for information in the library is the librarian. You should turn to the librarian whenever you need help answering questions such as, "Where can I find . . .?" and "Will you show me how . . .?" The librarian knows how to help you find what you are looking for. He or she will also gladly show you how to use the different types of reference tools.

The listing of reference works that follows does not include all that are available. However it is a sampling of those you will be using most often in the years to come. And you should get an idea from this listing of just how much variety there is in reference material.

INDEXES

An **index** is something that guides you to the specific information you are looking for.

You may already be familiar with the indexes in books, usually found at the back. They list for you, alphabetically, the names and subjects that appear in the book and on what specific pages this information can be found.

The *Readers' Guide to Periodical Literature* is an index to articles in **periodicals** (magazines). It lists articles alphabetically by subject and by author. You will find near the front of each volume a list of the periodicals that are indexed.

Also at the front of the *Guide* will be an explanation of how to read the information as well as a key to the abbreviations used throughout. Each volume of the *Guide* covers a particular time period that is clearly marked.

ATLASES

An **atlas** is a bound collection of maps, charts, tables, and other such materials arranged in an order chosen by the publisher and shown in the table of contents.

At the front of most atlases is a key showing the symbols used in the atlas and an explanation of what each symbol means. An airplane, for example, may show the location of an airport.

A current atlas, through its maps and charts, can also show

you such things as the annual rainfall in the Sahara Desert or the routes of railroads. An historical atlas can show you the movements of people as they have spread throughout the world or the approximate location of American Indian tribes at specific times in U.S. history.

Both Hammond Incorporated and Rand McNally publish many editions of their atlases, some designed especially for student use.

DICTIONARIES

A **dictionary** is an alphabetical list of words. It gives the meaning or meanings of a word, the way the word is pronounced, and how the word is used. Many dictionaries also give the origin of the word.

An unabridged dictionary is one that is not condensed or shortened from a larger dictionary. It will include almost all the words in a language. Abridged dictionaries contain the most commonly used words in a language.

In addition to giving the definition, pronunciation, and origin of words, a dictionary will have some charts, tables, and even small illustrations to depict certain words. Most large dictionaries include several tables that can be found either in the main body of the dictionary or in a separate appendix. One table will give weights and measurements, another will list the currencies used throughout the world, for example.

Many dictionaries are limited to words that have special significance to a particular group, for instance, a medical dictionary. Foreign language dictionaries translate the words from one language into another. Biographical dictionaries include information about a particular group of people — perhaps Americans, women, or authors who write for children. Geographical dictionaries give information about places.

Typical of the general dictionaries published with the student in mind are the *Thorndike-Barnhart Advanced Junior Dictionary* and *Webster's New Elementary Dictionary*.

BIBLIOGRAPHIES

A **bibliography** is a list of works. It can be a book listing all the books and articles written by a specific author — Mark Twain or Louisa May Alcott, for example — or it can be a book listing all the books and articles that have appeared on a particular subject — dinosaurs, American Indians, or UFOs, for example.

Many nonfiction books have bibliographies at the end of the text. This lists all the printed material used by the author as a source of information.

DIRECTORIES

A **directory** in the library is a book listing names, addresses, or other information about a specific group of persons or organizations. It may list the names and addresses of newspapers, publishers, doctors, manufacturers, and so on.

ENCYCLOPEDIAS

An **encyclopedia** contains articles on a wide variety of subjects. Though some of the articles may appear long, they are in fact all much less than book-length.

Encyclopedias often come in many volumes and are usually arranged alphabetically. There is also often a volume (or two) that is just an index to the rest of the encyclopedia. This index will help you find material not given separate treatment.

Two encyclopedias compiled and written especially for children and young adults are *World Book Encyclopedia* and *Compton's Encyclopedia*. Both issue yearbooks annually to highlight important events. *World Book* has a separate Research Guide/Index volume, while *Compton's* has a Fact-Index in each volume.

ALMANACS

Almanacs are usually published once a year. They contain a calendar of days and a large amount of information about a particular subject. Some also provide material on the planets, on special days and holidays of the year, and tables of miscellaneous information on a variety of unrelated topics.

Two popular almanacs are *The World Almanac and Book of Facts* and the *Information Please Almanac*.

The *World Almanac* has its general index in the front of the book, with a quick-reference index at the back. *Information Please* has a table of contents at the front and a comprehensive index at the back.

THESAURUSES

Thesaurus means a storehouse or treasure. A **thesaurus** is a book of words and their synonyms (words that have similar meanings) and/or antonyms (words that have opposite meanings).

Two of the most commonly used thesauruses are *Roget's Thesaurus of English Words & Phrases* and *Funk & Wagnall's*

Modern Guide to Synonyms and Related Words. Some editions of *Roget's Thesaurus* are arranged by categories that are based on the idea or intended meaning of the word. An index refers you to the proper category. *Funk & Wagnall's Guide* is written in essay form. It explains the differences and shades of meanings among synonymous words. The book is arranged alphabetically and has an index. For certain words antonyms are given.

BOOKS OF QUOTATIONS

Books of quotations vary widely in their selection and arrangement of material. One may give quotes from the writings of only one author, while another may include the speeches of a variety of different speakers. Some are arranged by topic and others are arranged chronologically. Two examples are *Bartlett's Familiar Quotations,* a collection of passages, phrases, and proverbs traced to their sources in ancient and modern literature, and Stevenson's *The Home Book of Quotations.* Both have excellent indexes.

VERTICAL FILE

The **vertical file** is a collection of pamphlets, pictures, articles, and documents temporarily in the library's collection. It consists of printed matter that will eventually be thrown out. This will happen, perhaps, when a book on the same subject appears or when the material becomes too worn for use.

Vertical file material may be kept in a special cabinet or case or may be kept in boxes. The library will have near the file an index to the material that indicates the topics or subjects to be found there.

INDEX

Alexandria, Egypt, 2
Almanacs, 56
Atlases, 53–54
Author entries, in catalog, 36, 37, 38, 41

Bartlett's Familiar Quotations, 57
Bibliographies, 41
Biographies, 19, 55
Book card, 18
Bookmobiles, 10
Borrower's card, 48
Borrowing, 8, 48–50
Branch libraries, 10

Call number, 41–44
Cataloging, 36–46
Card catalogs, 36, 39
Catalogs, 36–46
Charge Desk, 48
Checking out books, 48
Circulation Desk, 48
Classification systems, 18–33
    Dewey Decimal, 18–25
    Expansive Classification System, 28–31
    Library of Congress, 19, 28–33, 41
"Closed" stacks, 19
Classifying, 18–33

Codexes, 5
College libraries, 14
Compton's Encyclopedia, 56
County libraries, 10
Cuneiform language, 2
Cutter, Charles Ammi, 28–31

Dark Ages, 5
Dewey, Melvil, 20–22
Dewey Decimal System, 18–25, 41
Dictionaries, 54–55
Dictionary catalog, 36, 37
Directories, 55
Divided catalog, 36–37

Encyclopedias, 55–56
Entries, catalog, 36–45
Expansive Classification System, 28–31

Fiction, 9
    arrangement of, 20, 44
Film equipment, 48
Fines, 50
Foreign language dictionaries, 54
Franklin, Benjamin, 5
Funk & Wagnall's Modern Guide to Synonyms, 56–57

Geographical dictionaries, 55
Glossaries, 41

Harvard College, 5
History, library, 2–5
Holdings, library, 9–10

Home Book of Quotations, 57
Hospitals, 11

Indexes, 53
Information Please Almanac, 56
Interlibrary loans, 11

Jefferson, Thomas, 28

Learning centers, 14
Library card, 48
Library Company of Philadelphia, 5, 19
Library of Congress, 28
    Classification System, 19, 28–33, 41

Main entries, in catalog, 39–41
Media centers, 14
Metric system, 22
Microfiche; microfilm 36, 39
Middle Ages, 5

Nonfiction, 9
    classification of, 18–25, 28–33
Notations, 18
Numbers, of libraries, 2

"Open" stacks, 18
Overdue books, 50

Papyrus, 2–5
Parchment, 2–5
Periodicals, guide to, 53
Peterborough, N.H., 5–8
Philadelphia, 5, 19

[60]

Pompeii, 5
Prefaces, 52
Ptolemy I, 2
Public libraries, 8–11

Quotations, books of, 57

Rare books, 14
Readers' Guide to Periodical Literature, 53
Reference books, 9, 52–57
Registration cards, 48
Renewing books, 50
Resource centers, 14
Roget's Thesaurus, 56–57
Romans, ancient, 2–5

School libraries, 11–14
"See" and "see also" references, 45–46
Size, classification by, 19
Special libraries, 14–15
Spelling, Dewey and, 20–22
Stacks, 18–19

State libraries, 15
Stevenson's *Home Book of Quotations*, 57
Subject entries, 36, 37, 38–39, 44

Table of contents, in reference book, 52
Taxes, 5, 8, 10
Thesauruses, 56–57
Thorndike Barnhart Advanced Junior Dictionary, 55
Title entries, in catalog, 36, 37–38, 44

Unabridged dictionaries, 54
University libraries, 14

Vertical files, 57

Webster's New Elementary Dictionary, 55
World Almanac and Book of Facts, 56
World Book Encyclopedia, 56

ABOUT THE AUTHOR

JEANNE HARDENDORFF,
now a resident of New Ipswich, New Hampshire,
is a former associate professor of the
Graduate School of Library and Information Sciences
at Pratt Institute in Brooklyn, New York.
She is also a former librarian, having worked in
various capacities in libraries in Baltimore, Maryland;
Muncie, Indiana; and St. Louis County, Missouri.

Mrs. Hardendorff's current occupation is
free-lance writing. Over the last few years she
has had published a number of children's books,
including several retellings of folktales,
a song book, and two picture books.
In her spare time, Mrs. Hardendorff enjoys gardening
and tending to her two cats, Major and Minor.